Kinds of Blue

Kinds of Blue

Poems by

Sean Murphy

© 2024 Sean Murphy. All rights reserved.
This material may not be reproduced in any form, published,
reprinted, recorded, performed, broadcast,
rewritten or redistributed without
the explicit permission of Sean Murphy.
All such actions are strictly prohibited by law.

Cover design by Shay Culligan
Cover image by Justen Ahren

ISBN: 978-1-63980-502-0

Kelsay Books
502 South 1040 East, A-119
American Fork, Utah 84003
Kelsaybooks.com

For Justen Ahren: thank you being a creator, a facilitator, and a friend

Acknowledgments

Thank you to the following publication, in which versions of these poems previously appeared:

805 Lit + Art: "Marvin Hagler's Head"

Bethesda Urban Partnership Review: "Butch Warren's Beatitudes"

Beltway Poetry Quarterly: "Sam Cooke's Song"

The Daily Drunk: "John Belushi's Bungalow"

The Decadent Review: "Richard Pryor's Fire"

Decolonial Passage: "Pharoah Sanders's Exchange"

Contents

Opening Salvo: How to Talk About Jazz	13
Butch Warren's Beatitudes*	15
Alan Lomax's Archaeology*	16
The Killer's Compromise*	17
Sam Cooke's Song*	18
Pharoah Sanders's Exchange*	19
Duke & Trane's Turnaround*	20
Eric Dolphy's Departure*	21
Thelonious Monk's Moment*	23
Sonny Rollins's Rumble*	25
Jaki Byard's Experience*	27
Albert Ayler's Vision*	28
Intermission: Back to the Future	30
Marvin Gaye's Emergency*	31
Sly's Quiet Riot*	33
Popeye's Porkpie Hat	34
Fred Wesley's Revelation*	35
Joe Frazier's Jungle*	36
William Friedkin's Faith*	38
Disco's Last Dance	39
LKJ's Independant Intavenshan*	41
Loretta Lynn's Lungs	42
Francesca Woodman's Failure*	43
John Belushi's Bungalow*	45
Richard Pryor's Fire*	47
Marvin Hagler's Head*	51
Achilles's Last Stand	53
Orrin Keepnews's Discord	54
David Ware's Memories*	55
Matthew Shipp's Math	56
Charles Gayle's Commission	57
Parting Shot: The Shape of Jazz to Come	58

The power of music that poetry lacks
is the ability to persuade without argument.
—William Matthews

The copycats make money, but they're not the ones making
their own vistas. I'm into making vistas.
—Sam Rivers

Opening Salvo: How to Talk About Jazz

> "I'll play it first and tell you what it is later."
> —Miles Davis

How to talk about jazz music? The first step's establishing how *not* to talk about it. Second, lose the evangelical vibe: the stakes are so small—even though this should be life or death for those with ears wide shut. The only hope is trust that hearing is believing. That's it, except for everything else making this music so perfectly impossible to describe, jargon being the enemy of art best expressed without it. Also: never forget that jazz offers a reminder of the ways fortune and karma are on friendlier terms with zip codes and family crests than talent or industry—or worse still, a kind of honesty incomprehensible to those fluent in spreadsheets and portfolios measuring moral trash swept out to sea the second the check clears—anti-matter dead on arrival, living off the good deeds of those not built to thrive in this morose arena where soul isn't material; wealth's measured by the weight of wallets & cars driven at the highest speeds to nowhere. Third: imagine jazz as a landscape you can't capture with a camera. But it's also nothing like that. Rahsaan Roland Kirk talked about *bright moments*—those sacred occasions, sometimes lasting only seconds, where one feels deeply connected to the music, the message, the soul of the messenger. Booker Little, only 23 and already being stalked like easy prey by everything unfair about Fate, named his final album *Victory and Sorrow,* a declaration of defiance as he died like an abandoned Gabriel, his horn signaling revelation even while the world crumbled around him. Ornette Coleman insisted there was *Something Else!!!!* and then spent several decades offering clues to satisfy unsoothed minds. *Let My Children Hear Music,* the mighty Charles Mingus hollered, like Moses holding up his stone tablets, already aware there was better money to be made elsewhere, the ears of this world always itching for easier sources of amusement.

Perhaps it will suffice then, to suggest that jazz is music is, finally, an escutcheon: a spiritual shield for those seeking protection from false prophets. Art is best understood as a succession of prayers already answered, their source a faith that requires no ceremony and is both shared and celebrated, without words.

Butch Warren's Beatitudes*

"Don't I have the right to be crazy if I want to be?"
—Butch Warren

That woman cleaning high rise offices after hours
once bellowed the blues in speakeasys, pimps roaming
the 'hoods in three-piece suits & tossing bills on stage
like alms in collection baskets, a religious ritual from
days when dead presidents could make cops colorblind.

This janitor the grade school kids call Pops is the best
bass player nobody ever heard, because only anointed
cats signed by labels cut records, & studio work wasn't
near enough to keep the heat on in Harlem, or anywhere
else you stopped to live when you weren't on the road.

The invisible man—catching mist from the car wash
slipstream—spent more money on cigarettes he smoked
between sets than he makes now in tips, split ten ways
with co-workers whose fingers get numb from buffing steel,
the same way he ceaselessly scrubs memories from his mind.

That defenestrated scarecrow sporting five coats and fewer teeth—
who now counts time conducting traffic for change, or stalking
a defunded psych ward—still hears cheers from sold-out gigs,
back when the Blue Note buzzed like a honeycombed fortress full
of kings & soldiers, all extracting honey from air sticky with gold.

---

* Butch Warren was an American jazz bassist best known for his work in the 1950s and 1960s. An addiction to heroin followed by extreme mental illness curtailed his music career and he was eventually diagnosed with paranoid schizophrenia. For years he alternated between hospitals and being homeless, working a series of odd, menial jobs.

Alan Lomax's Archaeology*

He covered this country, hauling cumbrous equipment
in and out of a well-traveled car: a pilgrim searching
for lost and found sounds, a preservationist sworn
to his quest—saving the sort of cultural artifacts
that years and obscurity erase, using machinery
to reconstruct a disappearing past; like a teacher
assigning a book without text, or a lineless map
for a country lacking the context to understand or else
appreciate: these jigsaw pieces that comprise the puzzle
of America (as described by its unofficial ambassadors),
treasure buried in dialect and a market value that is,
like all cultural cache, impossible to assess using
the soulless barometer of what most folks will pay for.

---

* Alan Lomax was an ethnomusicologist, archivist, writer, scholar, oral historian, and political activist who collected thousands of field recordings of 20th century folk music.

The Killer's Compromise*

Tall and strong like an apple tree that starts
to shaking, until the branches sway—dropping
like so many uncoiled curls, whispering songs,
and who can prove what that serpent promised—
its fruit spread out to be saved, at least savored
before frost falls over the garden, this deal done
gone like the wind that shook our whole scene.

And if that's all too much to swallow, consider
The Killer, in his glorified prime, short-lived
like the freshest pie on the farm, a fool to think
this was Eternity, God not about to give last call
until the bar was empty and each drop of sweat
fallen like the original sin required to sing blues
so sweet even the Devil's eyes wouldn't stay dry.

This good old boy knew his bible so you couldn't
tell him kings didn't marry their cousins—and how
love of wine and women isn't the oldest story
in that book. Hell? If we're all made in His image
preachers should at least keep their story straight,
talking like they know about great balls of fire
or living off the grid, rocking & rolling that stone.

He was here to testify, talking on the record about
giving good as getting, old hounds and bullet holes
in the walls, cracked windshields and flattened tires,
fist fights and the kinds of pills pharmacists won't
sell, empty bottles and seeing them carry the coffins
of critics and competitors. The Devil's Music? Shit,
it's not worth singing about if it doesn't leave a scar.

* Jerry Lee Lewis, nicknamed "The Killer," was a rock music trailblazer, combining country, rockabilly, and his high energy piano prowess. After the hits "Whole Lotta Shakin' Goin' On" and "Great Balls of Fire" catapulted him to fame, his career derailed when it was discovered he'd married his 13-year-old first cousin in 1957.

Sam Cooke's Song*

Even during the worst of the day's decalescence
they sang, in defiance of the sun or else the song
itself, interrogating all those slights and sleights
that conspired to put them on the roads they built,
black links sweating in bracketed chains, indivisible.

They sang, effecting a fleet and curious indemnity,
compensation for uncountable hours, life's labors
lost or stolen, dissecting the unspoken or unspeakable
schemes: nameless and numbered, diseases contrived
as symptoms, sentences handed down like inheritance.

Even still they sang—coded texts for torn-out tongues,
the savage air aglow with conviction, an eloquence
unheard inside court rooms, their cells, or their selves,
appeals indicting this shame, adjourning all judgment
and seeking recourse in words—free as they'd ever be.

---

* Singer-songwriter Sam Cooke's song "Chain Gang," inspired by a chance meeting with an actual chain gang of prisoners on a highway, was released in July, 1960, becoming his second-biggest American hit.

Pharoah Sanders's Exchange*

Be wary of anyone filled with confidence,
insisting that everything was better before
the world went insane, suddenly too small
to satisfy the untold exigencies we inherit.

For one thing, humankind has always been
unbalanced: people with skin in the game
seldom tire of telling us it's good business
having the powerful slice the pie of society.

And few of us feel unfairness more keenly
than artists caught between buying bread
and selling their souls, our markets incapable
of sustaining those who bear beautiful gifts.

To create one needs to live, and staying alive
means feeding the machine, so it's impossible
to find peace, unless you abandon your Self—
believing that The Creator Has a Master Plan.

---

* In 1962, the composer and saxophonist Pharoah Sanders moved to New York City to advance his career; he struggled to find steady work and was homeless at times, occasionally selling his blood for money to buy food.

Duke & Trane's Turnaround*

It's as though two great war lords from different epochs, each having amassed a lifetime of campaigns—carnage and spoils beyond what any god or country could claim—find each other on a new and foreign field, nothing but instinct guiding the instruments at their disposal, muscle memory and a solemn invocation, inviting spirits and memories or anything sacred: as this battle march begins their many massacres are relived but backwards; all at once scores of deafened ears startle to the sound, still-bleeding bodies rise and rush in reverse toward quiet countries, putting down swords and finding homes and families, returning to domestic toils, modestly prepared meals slowly savored, cattle and fowl by the dozens withdraw from knives and axes to rejoin their herds, huddling safely in a morning mist; children do daily chores and are born in succession, husbands wed then hold their wives for the first time, become boys learning from older brothers to scrape whiskers from hardened chins, are shown how to ring bells at evening services for blessing of the crops, meditating upon—and still believing in—eternity, conjuring the magic of chanted spells, shrinking within themselves to look up expectantly at fathers dumb with adoration, and further on finally into a sweet, silent space, basking sightless and blissful in the warm calm of those moments following the divine light that brings life.

---

* *Duke Ellington & John Coltrane*, released in 1963, is recognized as a masterpiece and document of the legendary bandleader and the saxophonist, both representing their respective generations as the most revered and beloved musicians in jazz.

Eric Dolphy's Departure*

It sounds like an alien
transmission, today.

God only knows how
this reverberated with
inexperienced ears—
even in an era
when the world was
being reimagined,
seemingly each second.

Ecstatic and uncanny,
audacious and strange,
this is music
as mission statement:

*We are here to do work
and it's as serious as life.*

There was certainly something
in the air: America waking up,
slowly, from the old school
slumber of our whitest world.

And here were notes
giving expression to it
all—the pain and profundity
of being free enough
to die making a living
the worst way imaginable;
America undefeated
at finding new ways
to shun the ones who dare

describing the sublimity
of life, with burning words
that *had* to come from space
—or somewhere further out.

* "Something Sweet, Something Tender" is the second track of Eric Dolphy's 1964 masterpiece *Out to Lunch*, released months before his untimely death—from undiagnosed diabetes—at the age of 36.

Thelonious Monk's Moment*

It was finally happening: Monk had arrived,
jazz has arrived—and not their father's shit,
but a wholly singular form of expression,
carried, of course, through the 20th Century
on the broad black shoulders that hustled
their weapons of choice in & out of clubs:
brined with sweat and the smell of smoke,
the filthy, delicious shock waves of money
and applause, every concert a new chemistry
being conducted live, after working hours,
all these elements substantiating eternity.

Here, at last, the Underground given voice
not requiring words, but speaking to things
America is never really prepared to hear
(*we shall overcome, by any means necessary*
etc.), white folks marching; it was finally time
for this country to discover itself—renaming
certain spaces from the inside out: a hard art
that meets you on your terms (wherever you are
or choose to believe), like music always does.

And then it was over: Britain invaded again,
waves launching a million ships, bringing 45s
and the flattery of imitation, a perfect recipe
some master chef had tinkered with in the kitchen,
adding some blues here and country there,
seasoned, always, with the sweat of slaves—
that ingredient screaming *Made in the U.S.A.*

Through the graded curve of history, hindsight helps
ugly beauty seem inevitable; you can't make soup
without preparing the stock: you need to let those bones
soak and eventually, as the broth simmers ceaselessly
on the back burner, even success seems conceivable.

And on the lower frequencies, busboys and poets
continue cleaning plates, pocketing spare change,
and scarfing down whatever the cooks serve up,
hot meals hastily savored: straight no chaser—
then a quick mirror check for the teeth and back out
to the dining room, where folks who keep the lights on
order aperitifs and inquire about today's specials.

---

* One of the iconic figures of the bebop era, Monk was critically acclaimed but, like many fellow jazz musicians, struggled to earn a steady living. After decades of dues-paying, he was featured on the cover of *Time* magazine in 1964. Poised for sustained success, Monk was instead derailed by mental illness and largely disappeared from the scene by the late '60s.

Sonny Rollins's Rumble*

This is a street fight for sure,
but instead of fists flying, or
well-rehearsed dance numbers
West Side style, it's a Battle
Royale for the permanent record.

(Accounts getting settled, too:
riding this new wave of jazz
from the mid-60s—free enough
to unlock your mind but also
undertow your ass out to sea.)

Four men in their locked cage
of a studio, way beyond blood
and sweat or tears, because
just about anyone can throw
a punch (outside a boxing ring

That is, the sweet science—
an implacable prince called Sugar
outboxing the Bronx Bull &
fixing himself for a crown
that never fit any other man

Quite as snugly); we wage war
from long distance these days,
while this throwback rumble's one
that involves a band of brothers
during darker days, when fields

Of fire were lit stateside—and not
just figuratively—burned bridges
never rebuilt, God declared dead
(and even if he wasn't there was
nobody else answering the bell),

So once again, we depend on art
to guide us through no man's land
where, for a moment, the only sound
that makes sense is a soundless fury—
the possibility of music played out.

---

* *East Broadway Run Down*, released on Impulse Records in 1967, is the last album recorded by Sonny Rollins before industry pressures led him to take a six-year hiatus. The twenty-minute title track represents one of his more notable experiments with free jazz, where the saxophonist plays an extended, surreal series of notes entirely through the mouthpiece of his instrument.

Jaki Byard's Experience*

Isn't somebody going to talk about this genius,
and how his solos sound like he was rewriting
our encyclopedia, but also the theory of relativity—
simultaneously—in black and white dialogue?

---

* *The Jaki Byard Experience*, released in 1969, teamed up pianist Byard and multi-instrumentalist Rahsaan Roland Kirk, two iconoclasts with encyclopedic knowledge of jazz history who incorporated the whole history of this music in their compositions.

Albert Ayler's Vision*

Would-be angels, rejected or returned
to earth, ever eager to share their secrets—
which, suspiciously, all sound the same—
tend to talk about that white light
we'll all stride into, transitioning
from *here* to *there,* the strangeness
of dead lovers and famous names
(now friends) guiding them forward,
toward some impossibly bright beacon.

And why does it always have to be white?
A white god with a white beard dressed
in white (never mind the poor souls
taught to run the other way whenever
they saw men in white robes), looking
like a slick car salesman saying *No way
I can make a better deal on this trade-in.*

Or consider the revelation of Malcolm X,
reading the dictionary from start to finish
as he bided time in the purgatory of prison,
unlearning what it takes to stay on the right
side of iron bars, figuring out as he did why
they say those who win write our history,
and why white makes right and the wrong
people get blackballed—according to a code
baked into words by the white pie in the sky:
a place where all will be revealed, baptizing
non-believers with the light of white, hot fire.

What did Albert Ayler see when he wept
into the East River, that night he disappeared
forever, having been driven more than halfway
to distraction by the voices that wouldn't stop,
and why didn't the Lamb of God put bread inside
his basket when he played the ecstasy of saints
marching in? Did he see a reflection—of himself
or the absent savior who died for our sins—or else
the void of all color & sound as a weary moon hid
behind the clouds (holy ghosts keeping off the record),
unwilling to witness one more force majeure
amongst martyrs, the Devil, and the deep blue sea?

* Avant-garde saxophonist Albert Ayler made albums at once decidedly—even provocatively—non-commercial, yet deeply spiritual and ecstatic, and like many other jazz musicians, despite being critically acclaimed, he ceaselessly struggled to make a living. In 1969 he wrote an open letter describing his apocalyptic visions and, after being asked why he was wearing a fur coat with his face covered in Vaseline in the summer heat, replied "Got to protect myself." Ayler was found dead in New York City's East River on November 25, 1970, a presumed suicide.

Intermission: Back to the Future

What if the jazz musicians who wound up in asylums or worse, who became broke and broken trying to furnish short cuts to the sublime, were like heroes in some movie, sent back through history to prepare us for a time when we'll find ourselves in some spiritual outback, a walkabout preparing us for a new and better stage of existence, and these unassuming gods are meant to guide us through this oblivion where serenity is scarce as water, and even though all the wrong people—the ones paid to adjudicate—dismiss them as insane, watching if not orchestrating while they are silenced or made to endure places inhospitable to their humanity; even as they're mocked and ignored, they press on with the calm certainty of volunteers committed to something more substantial than rewards found on this earth, their task more significant than death or destiny, because they're doing more than merely saving the world?

Marvin Gaye's Emergency*

Question: *What else is new, my friend?*

(Did you hear the one about how the Execs
signing the checks—anti-insight their M.O.—
didn't want to release *What's Going On*
when Marvin brought it to them
like the goose with the god damn golden egg,
and how it was less business or economics,
or the usual suspects being in charge,
but the fact that every so often when prophets appear,
seemingly out of nowhere, they're not only ignored
but shunned, and in the most extreme cases exterminated
(a family affair: an inside job between Marvin and his old man
involving blood, drugs, and a gun—so what could possibly go bad
besides everything?), yet we're getting ahead of ourselves,
because first he had to ask *What's Happening Brother*:
a song as series of queries which seem innocent enough
to be simple, but because they are being asked
amongst men, and this world is the way it is,
they are, in fact, emergencies—

(*hey baby, what you know good?*),
they are awkward
(*are they still getting down where we used to go and dance?*),
they are timely
(*will our ball club win the pennant?*),
they are topical
(*war is hell; when will it end?*) ,
they are everything
(*how in the world have you been?)*

—so who knew, including Marvin, he was The Man
at the right moment to let everyone know
what's been shaking up and down the line?

Especially since we're still asking these questions
today, money is tighter than it's ever been
and troubled men decide what's going on
across this land; so while we have these sounds
we know that's not enough—and will never be,
but it's more than we could ask or even pray for
considering there's far too many of you crying.)

Answer: *This ain't living; this ain't living.*

---

* The second track from Marvin Gaye's 1971 album *What's Going On,* "What's Happening Brother," was written for his brother Frankie about Vietnam veterans returning to the states and feeling disconnected from current events and American culture.

Sly's Quiet Riot*

It's that rainy day on his album cover: Marvin grim
but game to assess the contentious state of our union,
filtered through his own pains and pitfalls, always
able to perceive the sun skulking behind the clouds,
neither optimism nor acceptance, a sensibility shaped
by countless church sermons and street scenes; seeing
the goodness of exploited people trying to get over,
feeling flames closing in from all sides—America
a melting pot that takes the heat, absorbing ingredients
flavored with Luv N' Haight, but also Hope—we dug
this grave but can dig ourselves out, Everyday People
with a prayer and the hope: *I Want to Take You Higher.*

I'll tell you *What's Going On,* a face from our future says:
the American flag w/ spaced out stars, suffocated by its own
aberrations, one beloved child learning while another burns,
boys with bricks in their backyards sent into rice paddies
to reclaim the prizes empires always pay for, a subscription
that re-ups until peace time; then we get busy building
prisons to keep invisible men on the back burner, simmering
and setting their sights on one another like so many bugs
trapped in a bottle—scorching under the search lights, praying
for some rain to wash away the sins and this smell—Death
just a shot away and Time here to stay, like snow-blind poets
lost inside themselves, scarcely believing the things they see.

---

* Sly Stone intended to name his 1971 album *Africa Talks to You* but changed it to *There's a Riot Goin' On* as a response to Marvin Gaye's *What's Going On,* released earlier that year.

Popeye's Porkpie Hat

"He's a good cop, he's basically a good cop,
he's got good hunches every once in a while."
—Captain Simonson, *The French Connection*

There goes Jimmy Doyle, hitting the bricks like a tsunami of Irish Whiskey, scuffed wingtips and the adrenalized bluster of a bull in the China White shop, attracting stray dogs with some elbow grease and the crime scene of his unwashed ass. Those were the days, we say, but it's true—you could smell the Big Apple before you even saw it: a cocktail of cigar smoke, sweat, car exhaust, and fear. Fear that the city would stay dry, like some postmodern Prohibition. Fear of shaking down a sketchy pimp with a dirty needle in his drawers. Fear of rooftop assassins and fellow police. Fear of superiors and the officious gods who fuck with your incident reports. Fear of winter mornings on the day shift (night shifts too). Above all, fear you won't get what you live for: catching a case that renders time clocks and three squares ridiculous, a case that clarifies why you do this and what's at stake: chasing that train in a borrowed car, blowing through red lights and looking like someone lit a cherry bomb in your lap, sharing a fifty cent slice with your partner while watching some Frog eat a hundred dollar lunch & shitting on every thing you'd swear is sacred, playing cat and mouse in some fetid subway, the collateral damage of inconvenient bystanders and your cholesterol count, the incidental business of arresting criminals almost important as avoiding jobs that handcuff you to a chair, stapling signed copies of other men's work, and above all, keeping this world safe from pricks who pick their feet in Poughkeepsie.

Fred Wesley's Revelation*

It never hurts if you write an anthem
folks will dance with, like a date,
because you can heighten awareness
while shaking your ass: it's something
about freeing one's mind & Everything
following—like the beat bouncing
off a snare drum coiled so tight
it could choke the very color white.

And if you need a little cool wind
to take the edge off, Maceo's the man
for this job, always pleased to pay the cost
so James Brown could stay The Boss,
which he was and always will be.

But this particular sermon concerns
an instrument allergic to funk,
at least until Fred Wesley throws down
like a cop waiting at a speed trap—
except he's not handing out tickets,
he's doling out the soul like our lives
depend on it, which they do.

And if you're willing to wade in
these waters, you'll find yourself
baptized in blackness, your heart
on fire like the bush that burned
on the mountain, its gospel
speaking to and through Moses.

---

* "Blessed Blackness" is a track from the 1972 album *Food For Thought* by James Brown's backing band The J.B.'s, featuring drummer John "Jabo" Starks, sax/flute player Maceo Parker, and trombonist/bandleader Fred Wesley.

Joe Frazier's Jungle*

> "It will be a killer and a thriller and a chiller,
> when I get that gorilla in Manila."
> —Muhammad Ali

Before they finished the business
of almost killing each other,
there had already been a murder;
a fratricide, actually.

Ali, once called Clay, the stuff
God used to make men,
who'd benefited from his brother
Joe being his keeper, saving him
from the floating sting of ruin—
when The System turned on him
after he turned on it, declaring
as he did that no Viet Cong ever
called him that word no man should
ever say to another, especially men
the color you see when an opponent
across the ring puts out your lights.

Ali, who hated and fought anyone
who still called him Cassius, had the gall
to utter the unthinkable, telling anyone
who would listen, which was everyone,
that Joe was an Uncle Tom; then got down
in the gutter and called him a gorilla
(this after they had rumbled in the jungle,
calling to question the horror of metaphors).
And is a jungle with trees worse than the one
where even the baddest men on the planet
must keep out of the crosshairs, false modesty
a matter of course, if not survival?

So they settled it again, third time the charm,
spread out over fourteen rounds resembling
stations of the cross in one hundred and twenty
degree heat, a billion eyeballs watching them
as they stalked each other, with bragging rights,
some sort of justice, and the unblinking verdict
of history all on the scale; of course every student
of the fight scene can confirm that pride goes
before the fall, except when it doesn't—and men
behind your back throw in the towel, too much
irony for any warrior to withstand and stay sane.

But Joe, a fortress unto himself, took even this
on the jaw and carried on, comporting himself
with the calmness of a wounded beast roaming
the heart of darkness, almost blind and addicted
to the taste of blood, moving toward the next scrape,
instinct instructing the bravest that it's their scars
fortifying them for the final bell, that last battle
which is always a fight to the death.

---

* Muhammad Ali and Joe Frazier's third and final fight (each man had won one of the previous contests), billed as the "Thrilla in Manila," is considered one of the most exciting and brutal boxing matches ever—and won by Ali after Frazier's corner asked the referee to stop the fight before the 15th round.

William Friedkin's Faith*

"What do you mean you don't know?"
—Jackie Scanlon / Juan Dominguez, *Sorcerer*

Even the fat-cats still cashing residuals
will tell you: the way we tend to assess art
is backward, ranking achievement by box office
numbers & units moved, seemingly for lack
of other ways to decree who wins or loses.

We say money earned makes everything
impartial: it's sell or die; if you can convince
people to buy, your name becomes a brand.

Of course, chasing profits is often anathema
to the creative impulse; the impetus for story
is sharing or connecting, or to get something out
of one's system, a virus that no doctors or drugs
can remedy, scaling mountains by way of metaphor.

Whoever endures comes to understand: they must
suffer to realize an unfettered vision: it has to be
seized from the devils demanding their sacrifice.

The ones driven by unfathomable forces figure
having to eat, sleep, and shit is compromise enough;
once you begin watering down your dream all is lost.

Faith's found as one accepts the losses, trusting
the work, like water, finds it level, reaching those
it was made to serve, even if they don't understand it
and can't explain the attraction—it's only in this way
posterity arbitrates that which disappears or endures.

* Following the critical and commercial success of his films *The French Connection* and *The Exorcist*, director William Friedkin's *Sorcerer* was equal parts labor of love and obsession, including a difficult shoot that went overbudget, endangered the actors, and alienated the crew. Released the same month (in 1977) as *Star Wars*, it was a box office flop, but Friedkin still considered it his best work, and the movie has been reappraised as an overlooked masterpiece.

Disco's Last Dance

Death Before Disco, some of us said (others, opportunistic or at least disc jockeys, wore it on t-shirts—their sentiment as sincere as their lives weren't). In fairness, backlash after ubiquity is the American Way: whether it involves athletes or actors or pop culture icons writ large, we root for you until we decide you've had enough of whatever you've been given, be it fame, fortune, free love, or the whole unholy trinity. Also, Disco was the soundtrack to whatever was happening at Studio 54, that WASP's nest of iniquity where unapproachable people went to be seen doing things most of us would never do; where the incorruptible Pelé and unkillable Kissinger stood afro-to-asshole, Mick Jagger and other jagoffs waiting in the wings, full wallets muffling their falls on feverish Saturday nights. Envious and out of other options, we decided to despise them. Oh, and this musical style managed to be at once too black *and* too gay, making it that much easier to misunderstand and malign. But how many of us were hazily aware of a familiar undercurrent—resurfacing throughout the twentieth century like a contagious disease—that involved certain cultures and the imperative to stymie them? How many of us failed to grasp we were being fed a narrative almost too easy to swallow, all artificial and fattening, like our devotion to Hamburger Helper and Shake 'N Bake, which epitomized, we thought, our mothers' culinary game? We, who didn't realize Howard Cosell sported a toupée, blissfully oblivious to what this signified, and the greedy ways some men grasp at short-cuts to stay relevant past their shelf-lives. Or what Donna Summers really meant when she sang about feeling love, not to mention what the word love alludes to in pretty much all pop songs. Or that the Village People, no matter what costumes they put on, were clearly playing for the wrong team. Did Disco Balls burn too brightly, leaving the dance lines on Soul Train blinded by their light, so many sweaty deities in leisure suits? Did Walter Cronkite fail to warn us *that's the way it is* as a decade died down and, crazy from the summer heat or simply looking for an excuse, the geniuses running the White Sox (because of course) had an idea: Get a bunch of drunk guys in one spot and give them a target. We applauded the televised transmission of salty earthlings flipping 45s onto the field, winning one for the Gipper and clearing a safe space for synthesizers and drum machines. Like so many soldiers of misfortune, these Macho Men reclaimed the soul of our nation according to the Gospel of beer-fueled dumpster fires. Look again at this unpoliced line-up and notice history pointing in either direction: can't you see hidden men in hoods, rallying around a tree for a photo op, or a trucker's cap crashing onto a lunch counter, or a cop dropping his baton on another colored crime in progress, or enraptured folks in red hats receiving marching orders from another old man—unembarrassable with his specious hair and oversized suit—who once blew rails in Big Apple bathrooms, a veteran of the Disco Daze doing the YMCA on stage without irony, promising to provide everything God, spinning vinyl in the VIP section, hasn't gotten around to delivering?

* On July 12, 1979, "Disco Demolition" night at Chicago's Comiskey Part deteriorated into a near-riot: the 98-cent discount tickets for anyone who brought a disco record to destroy drew an overflow crowd, some of whom stormed the field, causing the game to be canceled.

LKJ's Independant Intavenshan*

Never forget: Empire was perfected
across the pond; the Brits beating
what they believed to be sense into
so many heads, all of which should
have been happy to receive wisdom
from men, bearing their pale burden.

Within this mess Linton Kwesi Johnson
took his licks, learning that kicking back
was better with one's tongue, better still
with a song, sharpened by the experience
of too often having one's skull smashed
while Di White Petty Booshwah watched.

Rebel music is the patois of the streets—
a way to deconstruct the tired charades
foot soldiers from the ruling class have sold
the underfed for centuries; you can't change
hearts 'til you rearrange brains: the truth
from a turntable is 33 revolutions a minute.

---

* "Independant Intavenshan" is a track from the 1979 album *Forces of Victory*. Linton Kwesi Johnson is a Jamaican-born, British-based poet, dub-artist, and activist. In 2002 he became the second living poet, and the only black one, to be published in the Penguin Modern Classics series.

Loretta Lynn's Lungs

Not black but gold
owing to an old man
and later a husband

Doing the dirty work
that declares its love
like a song never sung.

Francesca Woodman's Failure*

Let's talk a bit about art
and the ways it's appraised,
particularly in the states.
That is, the gatekeeping,
the judging; all the ways
the same people remain
in charge of rule-writing,
which includes fund-granting,
free marketing, life-saving.
And ask, again: why is it that
so many artists, already fragile
for all the familiar reasons,
are served so poorly by us—
as consumers and friends?
And let's make sure to include
the types of people who think
suicide is a failure, or the act
of incurably weak individuals,
unable or unwilling to battle
through the familiar moments
that darken everyone's doors
at various times, only more so;
not able to reconcile their selves
and a world seemingly too busy
to recognize, much less support
their recalcitrant commitment
to creating, despite or because of
the way reality always insists
on being, abetting those who thrive:
laughing at awful jokes, silent
instead of offering solidarity,
occasionally crying, of course—
but only once the damage is done.

* Francesca Woodman was a photographer known primarily for her black and white pictures, which often featured herself or female models. Increasingly dejected due to the lack of attention and support her work was receiving, she took her life, aged twenty-two.

John Belushi's Bungalow*

There's the L.A. we created and the one that creates us
where, after hours & when the paparazzi scurries back
to their holes (hive-minded parasites without whom,
admittedly, the Strip's frisson would cease to function,
devils' bargains made with angels' blood), in alleys,
half-dead hobos give head for anything on offer, as puffed
up producers slump in the back seats of chauffeured cars—
oblivious to who's going down behind these sordid scenes.

On March Fourth, blowing off steam with some Bolivian
marching powder, John Belushi blew it, a speedball sent
from hell to usher him into anti-eternity, where our martyrs
perish so they'll stay preserved in digital tombs, also known
as bodies of work—death by natural causes if one considers
the place: snow blind inside the Chateau Marmont, itself
unable to contain his capacity or answer his appetites; only
stars die so indelibly, burned black by their own brightness.

Who would have bet against Belushi being the odd man out,
when Robert and Robin popped in, receiving and/or recoiling
from his hospitality, pizza boxes and filthy laundry scattered
like bounced checks? (Williams, sad clown sui generis, stayed
high on his own supply, subsisting on that rare ether until
the air got too contaminated, hoisted at last on his own
affected petard; De Niro—part Bull, part Mafia Boss—able
to call his own shots, bearing the weight of his greatness.)

It's as though the 20th C. couldn't believe what it created,
our culture always emerging from wreckage of ruined lives,
the truth forever outstripping what any screenwriter could
concoct, keyed up with squalid material too real for TV;
the news a succession of coroner's reports, confirming all
we already know: it's intoxicating work if you can get it,
but those not built to last will have their souls devoured,
mourned at a safe distance by voyeurs cursed with long lives.

* On the evening of March 4, 1982, John Belushi—after a short period of abstaining from hard drugs—was holed up in a bungalow at L.A.'s Chateau Marmont hotel, in the midst of a significant relapse; before being found dead of an overdose the following morning he was visited at various points of the evening by drug dealer Cathy Smith, comedian Robin Williams, and actor Robert De Niro.

Richard Pryor's Fire*

(An Exegesis)

I.

Here's the thing about saints: they're seldom esteemed
until they die. What's lost in the transformation from sinner
to sublime is how they ascend, immortalized for the things
we watched them achieve, often what frightens or informs us.

II.

We worship them in death in direct proportion
to how much they electrify us, while we're alive.

III.

The suffering, we'll say, is entirely self-inflicted—
but the gift? God given. That's a hustle that never fails.

IV.

Point is, being a human simile, the thing describing
itself? That's a burden few humans are built to bear.

V.

Don't call it a comeback, nobody said—but we all saw
you: cheating Satan on that billboard above Sunset Blvd.

VI.

Not Jesus, so much (too many lesser contenders for that
peculiar crown anyway); more like Lazarus: I've returned
from the dead, you didn't say, being alive your epiphany:
you were blinded, but your gift was giving sight
to those who otherwise couldn't see the light.

VII.

Metaphor as miracle: you strode to the stage, parting
the crowd not like Moses or even Judas—just a man,
who'd outgrown the n-word and all that hocus pocus.

VIII.

You said the words we couldn't say.
You said the words *you* couldn't say.

IX.

Miracles, as Christ could attest, ain't easy;
every soul saved obliges you to die a little bit,
because not faking it is what it takes
to make them believe. Plus, you died
for your own damn sins, but you tried
to save as many would-be fools—hoping
for heaven in ways we pay for—as possible.

X.

Make no mistake: priests are employed to recycle
an inflexible script; snake handlers make it up
as they go, testifying in ways we only need to hear once.

XI.

Certain persuasions are taught to believe the pope
is infallible. Pryor's conviction? He was merely perfect;
neither appointed nor anointed—only inevitable.

XII.

On the Strip, a Last Supper of sorts:
disciples gathered round
and The Reverend Jesse in the house,
but the only man preaching on stage,
regal in red like the pope, or a pimp—
which is the rare word that can be both
ironic and off limits, at least in mixed company.

XIII.

Those of us acquainted with the actual world
and what it does to everyone have a weakness
for the fallen angels, especially those brave enough
to abide, burned up but not burnt out,
their odometers dizzy from spinning so fast
(but, we know, that's where the fuel comes from).

XIV.

Look at him transform right in front of us:
a lion, a wino, a gangster, a preacher, a pipe,
a little boy—also himself, a role he was born to play
but also one he should be forgiven if,
at times, it enervated him, even as the jokes
wrote themselves, like attorney's fees or obituaries.
This, you didn't say, is the story of my life.

XV.

Never mind the Devil, temptation always appears
when we're alone in the desert. The battle's over
the heart & mind; how it's won is what we do with
our gift while we have it—when the lights shine
brightest, being ready for another fight that ends
in seconds or, defying faith and fate, lasts forever.

---

* In 1982, Richard Pryor's *Live on the Sunset Strip* film was released, recorded from a stand-up set exploring his recent trip to Africa, his epiphany regarding use of the N-word, his drug addiction, and acknowledging his infamous freebasing debacle, described initially in the press as an accident, but in actuality a more than half-serious suicide attempt.

Marvin Hagler's Head*

i.

What's the sweet science
if not a series of experiments
where irresistible force meets
an immovable object?

But what if one object is moving
to meet something that won't
be moved unless the force becomes,
finally, unable to resist?

What if, under the brightness
of all the lights in Caesar's Palace,
a broken hand can't break
a hard man's head or heart?

ii.

Hearns's hook was pure
physics, an electrical storm
that left minds rewired:
unplugged and lights out.

Hagler's chin was not
unlike a mountain range,
requiring centuries of wind
to shift a centimeter.

iii.

Does the wave despair
when it throws itself
at the shore, then collapses
back into black depths?

Do the rocks rely on instinct,
or are they focused solely
on the forces that shape them,
made to endure everything?

Will the stars look down
in silence, ceaselessly in awe
of the ways Nature rages then rests,
content to have changed everything?

---

* Originally billed as "The Fight," the 1985 middleweight championship match between Marvin Hagler and Thomas Hearns is considered one of the most exciting in boxing history. During the furious exchange of blows in the first round, Hearns broke his right hand on Hagler's head.

Achilles's Last Stand

for River Phoenix

We all want to be Tristan, if not Achilles:
the world—and its women (or men)—
rolling out before them like so many placid waves;
specimens of Nature's experiment, sublime
proof that evolution, in theory, is unassailable.

Fate and every conceivable misfortune broken
like a thousand untamable steeds, life itself
some buffet of every vice, harmless as the clouds
that cover him like the sun, keeping weather and worry
away: golden and glowing, burning always without heat.

Most of us simply don't have the heart, or the hair
for it, and few of us could take those punches with impunity
or go that deep into the role, fighting everyone else's battles,
metaphors or the moral of a story—yet ceaselessly subordinate
to capricious gods who blithely revoke what they bestowed.

Orrin Keepnews's Discord

> Author's Note: The original, self-explanatory title of this poem is *When I once suggested to Orrin Keepnews that rock music replacing jazz in the mid-'60s was part of a natural progression, however unfortunate, and such artistic trends are inevitable in American culture.*

I was, of course, *correct,* and as a young man—
a young jazz fan—this was the important thing,
the only thing. How could I know I was engaging
in a tradition wherein the young usher the old
out of the room, like kids (invariably spoiled ones)
eager to remove their parents from the equation,
putting them in places where paid staff do things
they can no longer do for themselves, but once did
for their offspring, already busy forecasting the ways
prospective inheritances will bolster the family budget.

I was *right,* but thirty years later I finally understand
that being wrong is not, in fact, the worst thing:
it's being included, even welcomed, in the company
of cynics who measure themselves according to wisdom
received from an endless line of incurious sentinels,
certain of so much—mostly that the world will be there
when they open their eyes; that newcomers need to ask
permission to change it; that they won't be besmirched,
or dismissed, one day, by acolytes made in their image.

---

* Orrin Keepnews was a critic, record producer, and lifelong advocate for jazz music; he founded both the Riverside and Milestone labels and, among many others, worked with legends such as Thelonious Monk, Bill Evans, and Sonny Rollins.

David Ware's Memories*

(has time re-written every line?)

Circular breathing's almost impossible
to fathom: a technique practiced
over centuries and cultures: a method
of creating uninterrupted song, sounding
natural as breath itself, simple as life.

(we will remember)

A skill specially designed for moments
when no thought's required, improvising
as a way to survive: memory's execution
facilitating a stream that will overwhelm
death and counteract those things it takes.

(the way we were)

---

* Avant-garde saxophonist and bandleader David S. Ware honed his playing technique and style over decades of dedicated practice, mastering breath control to enable a seemingly superhuman endurance. His circular breathing can be savored during the ten-minute introductory solo on the standard "The Way We Were," from his seminal *Live in the World* album.

Matthew Shipp's Math

Music is not unlike mathematics:
a language to express the infinite,
sequences of sounds processing
this world's fractions and fractures.

Scientists describe the universe
as a series of numbers, celestial
algorithms orchestrated in space,
codes bypassing acculturated brains.

We blind our minds with dialectics—
all right angles and wrong answers;
art explores the perspicacity found
within the silence of unplayed notes.

Charles Gayle's Commission

Those he baptized came
to find him in the desert
where he was preaching
subsisting on the insects
he caught with his hands
emaciated and wild-eyed
but by all accounts robust
and seldom in need of sleep
nourished by those spirits
that visited him devouring
impurities that cause evil
energies transforming him
to a messenger needing little
except the fury of his faith
and a voice these strangers
understood having traveled
so they might bear witness
to an anguished joyful noise
that could save and restore.

* Charles Gayle was an American free jazz musician who—after decades of obscurity and extended periods of homelessness while he played saxophone in the subway and on street corners—found a measure of fame later in life, performing in costume as "Streets the Clown" and occasionally speaking during performances about his political and religious convictions.

Parting Shot: The Shape of Jazz to Come

I still remember everything about it. Fall semester, senior year. The more I learned at college, the more I understood how little I knew. Something, obviously, was working. I was prescient, or just plain lucky enough to sign up for an elective called "Introduction to Jazz." We'd gone through the century, decade by decade, and it got better as we went. Yes, Bebop was what I'd been missing all along without realizing it. But it was what came next, the more formless expression that started creeping out of the margins—like lava oozing through ancient stones—that portended obsession. Those names: Mingus, Monk, Miles. And then, as we tackled the topic of "free jazz," a dissident with the audacity to name an album *The Shape of Jazz to Come*: Ornette Coleman, the canary in the post-bop coal mine. Like all iconoclasts, initially greeted with indifference, then disgust, then fear. His compositions scoffed at convention, freak flags flying out of the underground into the avant-garde. I still remember how quiet the room was and how concerned my ears got: What *is* this? Like something I'd never heard or felt; a new language, a new sensation, a new way of seeing everything, that first amoeba slithering onto shore, nothing I'd ever known and all the things I now knew I needed. How is it possible, I thought, to make instruments scream in agony and shriek in joy, *at the same time?* I walked around campus after, the autumn sky all schizophrenic yet serene with colors. And those notes I couldn't get out of my head. This is it, I thought. This is music. This is addiction. This is love. This is the first day of the rest of my life.

About the Author

Sean Murphy is founder of the non-profit 1455 Lit Arts and directs the Story Center at Shenandoah University. He has appeared on NPR's *All Things Considered* and been quoted in *USA Today, The New York Times, The Huffington Post,* and *AdAge*. A long-time columnist for *PopMatters*, he has had work appear in *Salon, The Village Voice, Washington City Paper, The Good Men Project, Sequestrum, Blue Mountain Review,* and others. His chapbook, *The Blackened Blues,* was published by Finishing Line Press in 2021. His second collection of poems, *Rhapsodies in Blue,* was published by Kelsay Books in 2023. This collection, *Kinds of Blue,* is his third collection. His first short fiction collection is forthcoming in 2024. He has been nominated four times for the Pushcart Prize, twice for Best of Net, and his book *Please Talk about Me When I'm Gone* was the winner of *Memoir Magazine*'s 2022 Memoir Prize.

To learn more and read his published work, please visit:
seanmurphy.net
@bullmurph

www.ingramcontent.com/pod-product-compliance
Lightning Source LLC
Chambersburg PA
CBHW030915170426
43193CB00009BA/853